SHARKS!

Based on the series by John Tartaglia
Written by Margie Markarian

Houghton Mifflin Harcourt
Boston New York

© 2019 The Jim Henson Company. © 2019 Herschend Entertainment Studios.
JIM HENSON'S mark & logo, SPLASH AND BUBBLES mark & logo, characters
and elements are trademarks of The Jim Henson Company. All rights reserved.
The PBS KIDS logo and PBS KIDS © PBS. Used with permission. PBS KIDS and the
PBS KIDS logo are registered trademarks of Public Broadcasting Service. Used with permission.

Photo Credits:
Alex Mustard: pages 4, 6 (top), 7, 9, 12 (bottom), 14, 16, 19, 20, 21
Rudolf Svensen: page 5
Andy Murch: pages 6 (bottom), 10, 12 (top), 13, 18
Magnus Lundgren: page 8
Jordi Chias: page 17

All rights reserved. For information about permission to reproduce selections from this book,
write to Permissions, Houghton Mifflin Harcourt Publishing Company, 3 Park Avenue,
19th Floor, New York, New York 10016.

ISBN: 978-0-358-05609-6 paper over board
ISBN: 978-0-358-05610-2 paperback

hmhbooks.com

Printed in China
RRD / SCP 10 9 8 7 6 5 4 3 2 1
4500770653

Welcome to Reeftown!

I'm Splash. I love to explore!

I'm Bubbles. I love adventure!

This is Dunk and Ripple. We're the Reeftown Rangers. Today, we're going to get to know some sharks.

Did you know there are more than 400 species of sharks? They can be many different sizes, shapes, and colors.

whale sharks

great white shark

Whale sharks and great whites are two big sharks.

L.anternsharks are small sharks. They glow in the dark!

velvet belly lanternshark

Hammerheads have heads shaped like hammers!

1 Habitat: Where Sharks Live and Lurk!

Sharks live in oceans around the world.

Greenland shark

I saw this Greenland shark in the ice-cold waters of the Arctic Ocean. Brrrr!

cat shark

I swam with this cat shark in the warm waters off the coast of South Africa.

Bull sharks can live in oceans and rivers.
They are big and fierce.

bull shark

I'd rather visit my friend Zee.
She's a zebra bullhead shark.

I'm small
but mighty!

The ocean is a big place.
Some sharks live deep down,
near the ocean floor.

It's dark in the Deep!

goblin shark

nurse sharks

Most sharks live closer to the ocean's surface, near the coast or in the open sea.

The sun's rays make it brighter up there!

Physical Features:
Looking Sharp!

Like me, sharks use fins to swim and gills to breathe.

Dorsal fin

Gills

Pectoral fins

Makos are fast swimmers. They can swim up to 60 miles per hour!

Pelvic fins

Tail

mako shark

I'm a fish. Sharks are fish. But our skeletons are very different.

great hammerhead shark

Sharks have rubbery **cartilage** instead of bone. It helps sharks move fast and bend. Whoosh!

Shark skin may look smooth but it feels rough. It is covered with tiny, hard scales called **denticles**.

nurse shark

Wow! Denticles are like a suit of armor for sharks!

Sharks have many rows of teeth. As soon as one tooth falls out, another grows in its place. Sharks lose thousands of teeth a year!

shortfin mako shark

3 Behavior:
Shark Antics!

Sharks are ocean **predators**. They eat other animals. They use their senses of smell, sight, hearing, touch, and taste to hunt.

whitetip reef shark

A shark doesn't need to see **prey** with its eyes. They can feel other animals moving in the water. Sharks can even tell which direction a smell is coming from!

I'm never playing hide-and-seek with a shark. It always has the upper fin!

tawny nurse sharks

When a shark is curious about something, it swims in circles around it.

Right before a shark attacks, it hunches its back, raises its head, and points its fins down. Chomp!

lesser-spotted dogfish

A baby shark is called a pup. Most pups hatch from eggs. When pups are born they know how to swim, hunt, and take care of themselves.

It's not easy being a baby shark. They have to watch out for bigger sharks who might eat them!

Most sharks eat meat. They are **carnivores**.

Some sharks eat seals, sea lions, dolphins, small whales, seabirds, and fish.

hammerhead shark

Some sharks eat **plankton**. Plankton are tiny plants and tiny animals that float in the water. Sharks scoop up the plankton with their big mouths. Gulp!

basking shark

I'm staying hidden in the seagrass for a while!

Bottom-dwelling sharks enjoy eating clams, mollusks, and other shellfish on the ocean floor.

I'm lucky I'm a seahorse!

angelshark

whale shark

Sharks do not have a taste for people. Sometimes a shark mistakes a swimmer or surfer for a sea animal. But shark attacks on people are rare.

Sharks are at the top of the ocean **food chain**.

But sharks face dangers too. Shark hunting and pollution are big problems. Sharing what you know about sharks is a good way to help sharks!

We all play a part in the rhythm of the reef!

True or False?
Test Your Shark Smarts!!

1. Sharks only live in cold water. True False

2. A shark's skeleton is made of bone. True False

3. A shark breathes using gills. True False

4. Shark babies are called pups. True False

5. All sharks are big. True False

6. Shark attacks on people are rare. True False

Answers: 1-F; 2-F; 3-T; 4-T; 5-F; 6-T

Glossary

carnivore – An animal that eats meat.

cartilage – Tough tissue that bends. Your ears are made of cartilage!

denticles – Small, hard scales that protect a shark's skin.

food chain – Plants and animals that rely on each other for food. In an ocean food chain, fish may eat plankton, then seals eat the fish, and sharks eat the seals.

plankton – Tiny plants and animals that drift or float in water.

predator – An animal that eats other animals.

prey – An animal that is hunted by another animal for food.